Ikenaga 2 Jos Leys

"A relatively simple formula can generate immensely complex images." – Jos Leys

Student Activity Book

Finding Fair Shares

UNIT 7

Investigations
IN NUMBER, DATA, AND SPACE®

Editorial offices: Glenview, Illinois • Parsippany, New Jersey • New York, New York
Sales offices: Boston, Massachusetts • Duluth, Georgia
Glenview, Illinois • Coppell, Texas • Sacramento, California • Mesa, Arizona

The Investigations curriculum was developed by TERC, Cambridge, MA.

This material is based on work supported by the National Science Foundation
("NSF") under Grant No.ESI-0095450. Any opinions, findings, and conclusions or
recommendations expressed in this material are those of the author(s) and do not
necessarily reflect the views of the National Science Foundation.

Finding Fair Shares

Investigation 3

Sharing One Brownie (page 1 of 2)

Cut up large brownie rectangles and glue the pieces below. Show how you would make fair shares.

1. 2 people share a brownie. Each person gets _____.

2. 4 people share a brownie. Each person gets _____.

3. 8 people share a brownie. Each person gets _____.

Sharing One Brownie (page 2 of 2)

4. 3 people share a brownie. Each person gets _____.

5. 6 people share a brownie. Each person gets _____.

Factor Pairs

For each number below, list as many factor pairs as you can.

NOTE Students practice multiplication combinations ("facts") by finding pairs of factors for a given product.

1. Example: 18

__2__ × __9__

__3__ × __6__

_____ × _____

2. 12

_____ × _____

_____ × _____

_____ × _____

3. 36

_____ × _____

_____ × _____

_____ × _____

_____ × _____

4. 16

_____ × _____

_____ × _____

_____ × _____

5. 40

_____ × _____

_____ × _____

_____ × _____

6. 24

_____ × _____

_____ × _____

_____ × _____

_____ × _____

Things That Come in Groups

Solve the story problems below. Write a multiplication equation for each problem and show how you solved it.

A package of popsicles has 6 popsicles.

1. How many popsicles are in 2 packages? _____

Example: Equation: _____ $2 \times 6 =$ _____

2. How many popsicles are in 4 packages? _____

Equation: _____

3. How many popsicles are in 8 packages? _____

Equation: _____

Finding Halves

Draw a line to create $\frac{1}{2}$ of each picture.
Label each half you create.

NOTE Students are
learning that half of an
area is 1 of 2 equal pieces.

SMH 56, 57, 58–59

1.

2.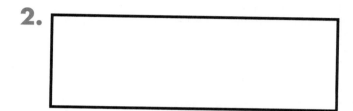

3.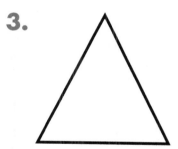

4.

Finding Thirds

Draw lines to create $\frac{1}{3}$ of each picture.
Label each third you create.

NOTE Students are learning that $\frac{1}{3}$ of an area is 1 of 3 equal pieces.

SMH 56, 57, 58–59

1.

2.

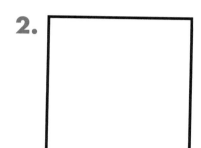

3.

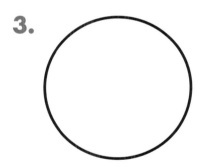

4.

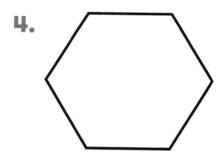

Ongoing Review

5. Which fraction is one half?

A. $\frac{2}{1}$ **B.** $\frac{4}{2}$ **C.** $\frac{1}{2}$ **D.** $\frac{1}{4}$

Sharing 12 Things

Solve each of these problems and show how you figured out your answers.

1. Oscar picked 12 apples. He gave $\frac{1}{3}$ of the apples to Gil and $\frac{1}{3}$ of the apples to Becky. How many apples did each of them get?

2. Pilar picked 12 apples. She gave $\frac{1}{4}$ of the apples to Dwayne, $\frac{1}{4}$ of the apples to Murphy, and $\frac{1}{4}$ of the apples to Kelley. How many apples did each of them get?

3. Chiang picked 12 apples. She gave $\frac{1}{6}$ of the apples to each of her 5 friends. How many apples did each friend get?

Multiplication Combinations of 2s, 4s, and 8s

NOTE Students practice multiplication combinations ("facts"). They look for patterns in the 2s, 4s, and 8s combinations.

SMH 49–51

1. Solve these problems.

$1 \times 2 =$

$2 \times 2 =$ $1 \times 4 =$

$3 \times 2 =$

$4 \times 2 =$ $2 \times 4 =$ $1 \times 8 =$

$5 \times 2 =$

$6 \times 2 =$ $3 \times 4 =$

$7 \times 2 =$

$8 \times 2 =$ $4 \times 4 =$ $2 \times 8 =$

$9 \times 2 =$

$10 \times 2 =$ $5 \times 4 =$

$11 \times 2 =$

$12 \times 2 =$ $6 \times 4 =$ $3 \times 8 =$

2. What patterns do you notice?

3. Ask someone at home to help you practice the multiplication combinations that you are working on.

What Fraction Is Shaded?

Look at each rectangle below. Label the fraction that is shaded.

NOTE Students determine what fraction of the whole rectangle is shaded.

 57, 58–59

1.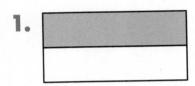

_____

2.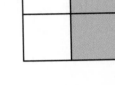

_____

3.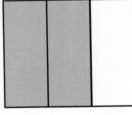

_____

4.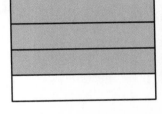

_____

5.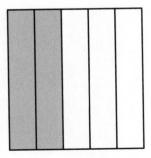

_____

Sharing Several Brownies

_____ brownies shared by _____ people

number of brownies   number of people

Draw a picture to show your solution or
explain in words how you solved the problem.

How many brownies does each person get? _____

Guess the Rule with Number Pairs

NOTE Students look for multiplication relationships between numbers in a table.

Can you figure out the rule for each table below? For each table, fill in the missing numbers and write the rule. Make sure that the rule works for all of the numbers in each table.

1.

⊠	△
3	15
6	30
2	10
4	___
10	___
___	35

What is the rule? _____

2.

⊠	△
4	32
2	16
5	40
3	___
6	___
___	8

What is the rule? _____

3.

⊠	△
4	24
2	12
5	30
3	___
6	___
___	42

What is the rule? _____

4.

⊠	△
9	3
21	7
33	11
12	___
30	___
___	9

What is the rule? _____

Are These Equal?

Answer these questions. Show your work.

NOTE Students use drawings or stories to show whether these fractions are equivalent.

SMH **63, 64**

1. Does $\frac{1}{2} = \frac{2}{4}$? _____

Show how you know:

2. Does $\frac{1}{2} + \frac{1}{2} = \frac{2}{4} + \frac{2}{4}$? _____

Show how you know:

3. Does $\frac{1}{8} + \frac{1}{8} = \frac{1}{4}$? _____

Show how you know:

Sharing Many Things (page 1 of 2)

Solve these problems and show your solutions.

1. There are 6 brownies on a plate. Four people share them equally. How many brownies does each person get?

2. There are 3 apples in a bag. Two people share them equally. How many apples does each person get?

3. How much is $\frac{1}{4}$ of 8 pies?

Sharing Many Things (page 2 of 2)

4. How much is $\frac{2}{3}$ of 9 marbles?

5. I have $\frac{1}{3}$ of $15.00. How many dollars do I have?

6. How much is $\frac{3}{4}$ of 32 color tiles?

© Pearson Education 3

Finding Fair Shares

Daily Practice

Identifying and Naming Fractions

NOTE Students identify and name fractions of rectangles.

 58–59

Name the fraction that is shaded.

1.
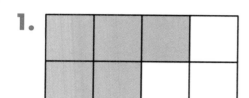

_____

2.

_____

3.

_____

4.

_____

Ongoing Review

5. Is this true or false? $\frac{1}{4} + \frac{1}{2} = 1$

   A. true   **B.** false

Hexagon Cookies

Use pattern blocks. Show all the ways to make
1 whole cookie. Have you found them all?
Are any of your designs the same?

Multiplication Picture Problems

NOTE Students practice solving multiplication problems.

 40–41

For each problem, draw a picture to represent the problem and then solve the problem.

1. $8 \times 3 =$ _____

2. $6 \times 6 =$ _____

3. $7 \times 4 =$ _____

How Many Legs?

NOTE Students solve multiplication and division problems in story problem contexts.

 SMH 40–41, 48

Birds have 2 legs.
Dogs have 4 legs.
Ladybugs have 6 legs.

1. There are 48 legs and they all belong to dogs.
How many dogs are there?

2. There are 48 legs and they all belong to
ladybugs. How many ladybugs are there?

3. There are 3 ladybugs, 7 dogs, and 11 birds in
the house. How many legs are there altogether?

Smallest to Largest

For each set of rectangles below, label the shaded part as a fraction of the rectangle. Then write the fractions in order from smallest to largest.

> **NOTE** Students practice putting unit fractions in order from smallest to largest.
>
> **SMH** 58–59

Set 1

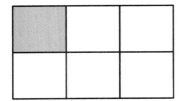      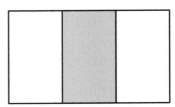

_____   _____   _____

From smallest to largest: _____ _____ _____

Set 2

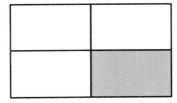   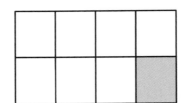   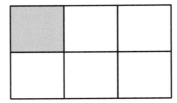

_____   _____   _____

From smallest to largest: _____ _____ _____

Choose one of the sets above and tell how you figured out the order from smallest to largest.

Many Ways to Make a Share

Think of sharing brownies or hexagon cookies.
Write all the fractions you know that work.

1. Ways to make 1 whole	**2.** Ways to make $\frac{1}{3}$
3. Ways to make $\frac{1}{4}$	**4.** Ways to make $\frac{1}{2}$
5. Ways to make $\frac{3}{4}$	**6.** Ways to make $\frac{2}{3}$
7. Challenge: Ways to make $\frac{5}{6}$	**8. Challenge:** Ways to make $\frac{5}{8}$

Fractions of a Group

Solve these problems and show
your solutions.

NOTE Students solve problems
about sharing objects equally.

 56, 60

1. How much is $\frac{3}{5}$ of $10?

2. There are 12 computers in the lab. $\frac{3}{4}$ are being
used by students. How many computers are
available for others to use?

3. I have 6 erasers and gave $\frac{1}{3}$ to my friend. How
many erasers did I give her?

Ongoing Review

4. Oscar had 9 pencils and gave $\frac{1}{3}$ to his sister.
How many pencils did he have left?

   A. 2   **B.** 3   **C.** 5   **D.** 6

Triangle Paper

Feeding Animals

Solve the following story problems and
be sure to show your work.

NOTE Students practice solving
multiplication and division problems
in story problem contexts.

SMH 40–41, 48

1. At one stable, horses are fed carrot
sticks each morning. Each horse eats 6 carrot
sticks. How many carrot sticks will 4 horses eat?

2. Horses also like to eat apple slices as treats. The
stable keeper has 48 apple slices for 4 horses.
How many apple slices will each horse get if
they are shared equally?

3. Fuzzy is the pet rabbit in Ms. Tham's classroom.
Fuzzy eats 3 lettuce leaves each day.

   a. How many leaves will Fuzzy eat in 6 days?

   b. How many leaves will Fuzzy eat in 9 days?

Equal Shares

Answer each question below, and show how you figured it out.

NOTE Students use what they have been learning about fractions as equal parts to answer questions about making equal shares.

SMH **57**

1. How can 4 people share this corn bread equally? What would each person's share be?

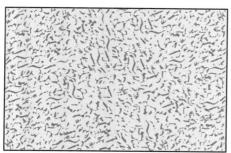

2. How can 5 people share this corn bread equally? What would each person's share be?

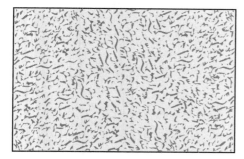

3. How can 10 people share this corn bread equally? What would each person's share be?

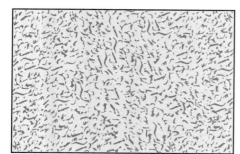

Other Things to Share

How would you share each of the following? Make equal shares if possible. If equal shares are not possible, decide what you would do. Show your thinking for each.

1. 9 brownies shared among 4 people

2. 9 balloons shared among 4 people

3. 9 dollars shared among 4 people

4. Solve this problem on a calculator: $9 \div 4$

Sharing Dollars

Solve the following problems. Show how you solved each.

1. Suppose that 4 friends share $1.00 equally. How much money will each one get?

2. How much would each person get if 4 friends shared $2.00 equally?

3. How much would each person get if 8 people shared $2.00 equally?

4. How much would each person get if 4 people shared $5.00 equally?

Name _____   Date _____

Finding Fair Shares

Daily Practice

Missing Factors

Fill in the missing factors in these problems.

NOTE Students practice multiplication combinations ("facts") in related sets.

1. $6 \times \underline{} = 24$ $6 \times \underline{} = 36$	**2.** $5 \times \underline{} = 35$ $5 \times \underline{} = 45$	**3.** $\underline{} \times 12 = 36$ $\underline{} \times 12 = 48$
4. $9 \times \underline{} = 27$ $9 \times \underline{} = 36$	**5.** $\underline{} \times 7 = 21$ $\underline{} \times 7 = 42$	**6.** $3 \times \underline{} = 24$ $3 \times \underline{} = 30$
7. $\underline{} \times 8 = 32$ $\underline{} \times 8 = 40$ $\underline{} \times 8 = 48$	**8.** $3 \times \underline{} = 9$ $5 \times \underline{} = 25$ $7 \times \underline{} = 49$	**9.** $\underline{} \times 4 = 28$ $\underline{} \times 4 = 36$ $\underline{} \times 4 = 44$

Many Ways to Make a Whole

For each hexagon below, write the name of the fraction on each piece. Then write an equation to show what fractions make the whole.

NOTE Students practice naming fractions and combining them to make one whole.

 58–59, 64

1.

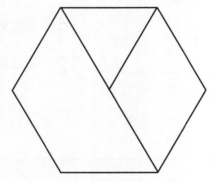

Equation: _____

2.

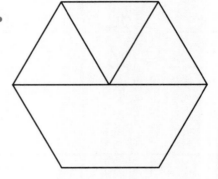

Equation: _____

3.

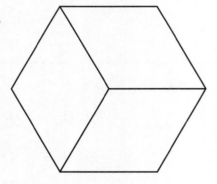

Equation: _____

Sharing With and Without a Calculator (page 1 of 2)

Solve each of the problems below. First solve the problem without using a calculator and show how you figured it out. Then solve it with a calculator.

1. When 2 people share $3.00 equally, what is each person's share?

One person's share: _____

Calculator answer: _____

2. When 4 people share $3.00 equally, what is each person's share?

One person's share: _____

Calculator answer: _____

Sharing With and
Without a Calculator (page 2 of 2)

3. When 8 people share $6.00 equally, what is each person's share?

One person's share: _____
Calculator answer: _____

---

4. When 2 people share 5 brownies equally, what is each person's share?

One person's share: _____
Calculator answer: _____

My Own Sharing Problems

1. Make up a problem about equal shares so
that each person gets one half of something.
Show the problem and the solution.

For example: If 6 people share 3 apples, each
person will get $\frac{1}{2}$ of an apple.

2. Make up a problem about equal shares so that
each person gets one fourth of something.

3. Make up a problem about equal shares so that
each person gets three fourths of something.

Counting Around the Class

NOTE Students find the multiples of a given number and solve multiplication problems.

SMH 42

1. Ms. Jorge's class counted by 3s. The first person said 3, the second said 6, and the third said 9. How many people counted to get to 36? How do you know?

2. Mr. Snell's class counted by 8s. The first person said 8, the second said 16, and the third said 24.

a. What number did the 6th person say? How do you know?

b. What number did the 12th person say? How do you know?

3. Ms. O'Leary's class counted by 10s. The first person said 10, the second said 20, and the third said 30. There are 24 students in Ms. O'Leary's class. What number did the last person say?

More Equal Shares

Answer each question below, and show how you figured it out.

> **NOTE** Students use what they have been learning about fractions as equal parts to answer questions about sharing a pizza.
>
> **SMH** 57

1. How can 3 people share this pizza equally? What would each person's share be?

2. How can 6 people share this pizza equally? What would each person's share be?

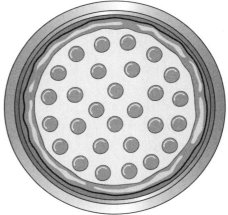

3. How can 12 people share this pizza equally? What would each person's share be?

Different Ways to Share

NOTE Students find ways to divide a group of objects equally.

SMH 60

Solve each problem. Draw pictures to help you explain your answer.

1. 2 people share 5 granola bars equally. How many granola bars does each person get?

2. 6 people share 8 waffles equally. How many waffles does each person get?

3. If 4 people share $2.00 equally, how much does each person get?

Ongoing Review

4. 6 people share 4 sandwiches equally. How much does each person get?

A. $\frac{1}{2}$ **B.** $\frac{1}{4}$ **C.** $\frac{2}{3}$ **D.** $\frac{3}{2}$

Turkey Sandwiches

Nick is helping his mother make sandwiches for a school outing. He has a loaf of bread, sliced turkey, and cheese.

NOTE Students consider the fractions of ingredients used and left over when making sandwiches.

 56, 57, 58–59, 60, 61–62, 63

24 ounces   21 ounces   8 ounces

1. To make one sandwich, Nick uses two slices of bread, which equal two ounces. What fraction of the loaf of bread does he use to make one sandwich?

2. Nick will use 3 ounces of sliced turkey for each sandwich. What fraction of the sliced turkey will Nick use to make one sandwich?

3. If Nick uses 1 ounce of cheese for each sandwich, what fraction of the cheese will he use for one sandwich?

4. How many sandwiches can Nick make if he uses 2 slices of bread, 3 ounces of turkey, and 1 ounce of cheese for each sandwich? What will he run out of first? Explain how you know.